The Mountain Bike Knowledge

by William Nealy

Menasha Ridge Press
Birmingham, Alabama

Published by Menasha Ridge Press
3169 Cahaba Heights Road
Birmingham, AL 35243
(800) 247-9437

Library of Congress Cataloging-in-Publication Data
Nealy, William, 1953-
The Mountain bike way of knowledge/by William Nealy.
p. cm.
ISBN 0-89732-097-2
1. All-terrain cycling—Caricatures and cartoons. 2. American wit and humor. Pictorial. I. Title.
NC1429.N42A4 1989 89-27655
741.5"973-dc20 CIP
Rev.

To my friend
John Dolbeare

1957 – 1989

Acknowledgements

Those without whom this book wouldn't have been possible... John Barbour, Lynn Brandon, Wayne-Bob Colwell, Mark Cwick, Dave Schmidt, Nantahala Outdoor Center, Bob Sehlinger, Henry Unger, Barrie Wallace, James Torrence, Tom Schlinkert, and "Bruce".

Very special thanks to my orthopaedist, Dr. Edwin Preston for patching me up every few months, to Gordon Sumerel and the Pedal Power bike shop for keeping my bikes running, and to Dr. Peter Perault for keeping me relatively sane.

Lastly and not leastly, eternal gratitude & love to my main muse, Holly Wallace...

Dear Dudes and Dudettes,

This is not a book about correct mountain bike riding technique. Fortunately for us, there is no such thing as "correct" mountain biking. Rather, this is a journal of my misadventures on mountain bikes over the last ten years, the reading of which may help you avoid some of my mistakes and perhaps even take a short-cut on the mountain bike learning curve.

Despite my cartoon portrayal of it, mountain biking is not an inherently dangerous sport. However, there are (like me) inherently dangerous mountain bike riders. If you ride out of control you will, like me, probably experience the karmic consequences of out-of-controlness in the form of concussions, separated shoulders, broken collarbones, cracked ribs, sprained wrists, 3rd degree road burns, and lacerations too numerous to mention.

It took me about nine years and a few kestrels' worth of medical bills to finally ascertain the precepts of safe, sane riding: ① Always wear a helmet! (I hate them too), ② Ride in control whenever possible (sometimes you just gotta hot dog!), ③ Seek to minimize your impact on the natural environment (repair trail damage, use established trails, don't shred meadows, etc.), ④ Refrain from running into, spooking, and/or alienating pedestrians, hikers, horses, horse people, and wildlife, ⑤ keep a well-lubed chain, and ⑥ Have as much fun as you can reasonably tolerate!

Kowabunga,

W. Nealy

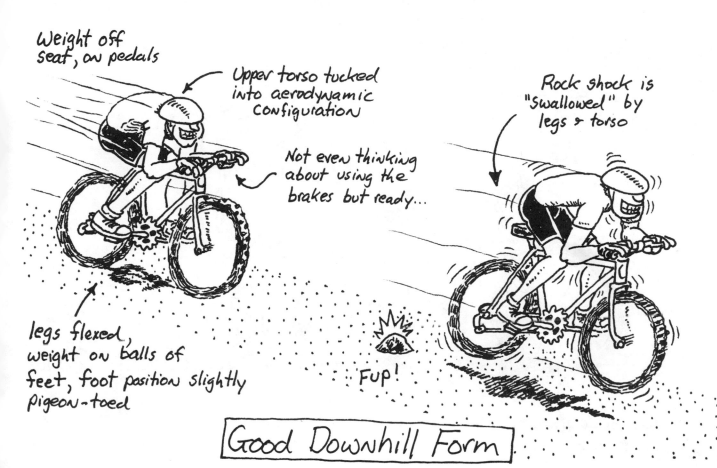

Good Downhill Form

Mtn. Bike "All The Way"

① Take a good quality mountain bike...

Cost $725.⁰⁰
Weight 28 lbs.

A defense contractor approach to a more sophisticated all-terrain all-aspect individual-rider two-wheeled personnel carrier.

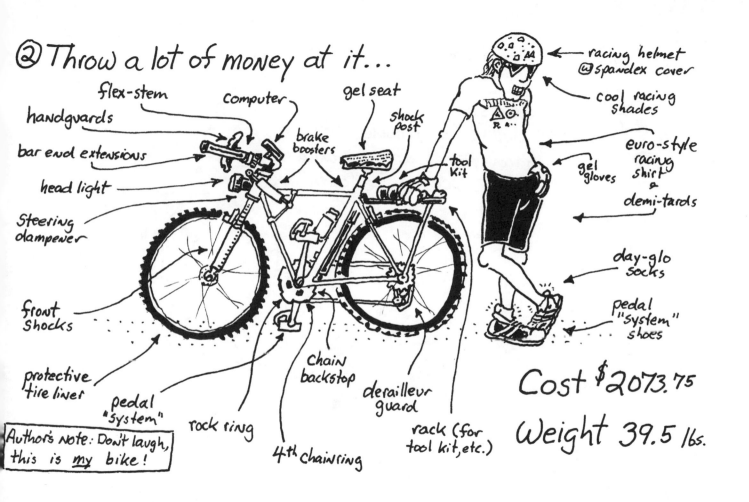

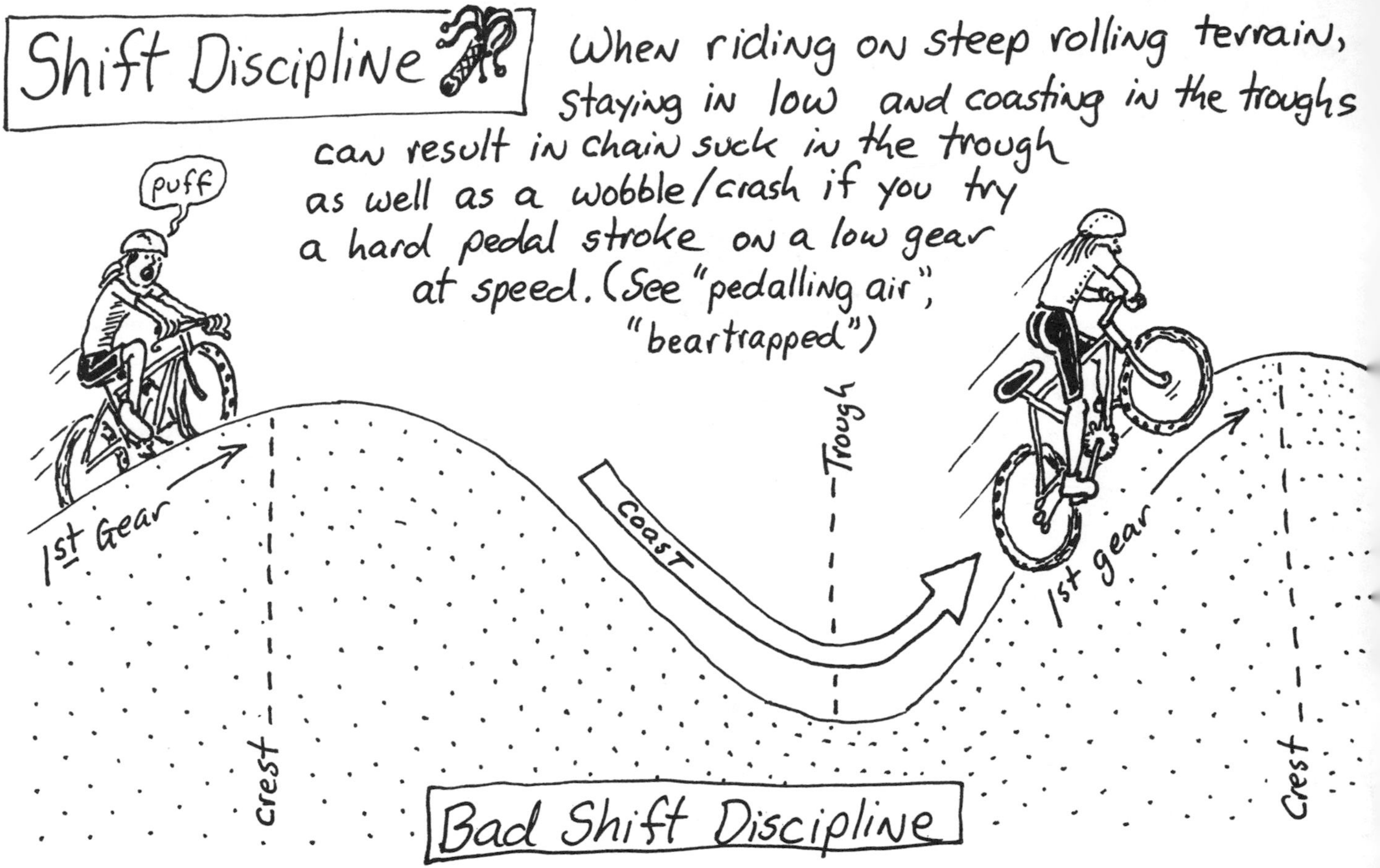

Shift Discipline — When riding on steep rolling terrain, staying in low and coasting in the troughs can result in chain suck in the trough as well as a wobble/crash if you try a hard pedal stroke on a low gear at speed. (See "pedalling air", "beartrapped")

puff

1st Gear

Coast

Trough

1st gear

crest

Crest

Bad Shift Discipline

To lessen the chances of chain suck in the trough and/or injury to your naughty parts by pedalling air, use your gears...that's what they are there for. Under almost all conditions, use the highest gear possible.* (See "Pedalling Air")

* Obviously I'm not saying to use every gear on each and every little hill, just the gear appropriate to your velocity on average.

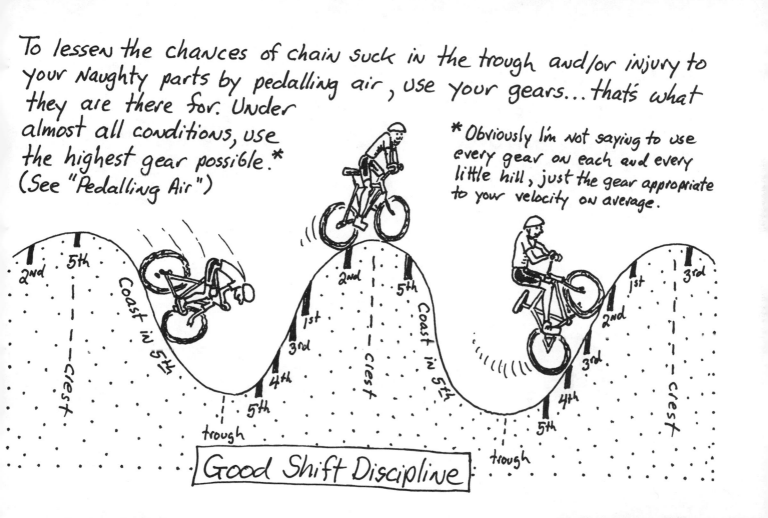

Good Shift Discipline

Scream (skrēm) v. To achieve a velocity such that all rules of common sense and safety are thoroughly violated. Penultimate Fun! (a.k.a. "Bomb")

Word Derivation; As in "Too scared to scream"

Screaming a Hill

Poled (pōl·d) v., To be abruptly separated from one's mountain bike by a free-standing horizontal object lying parallel to path of bike. See "First Aid".

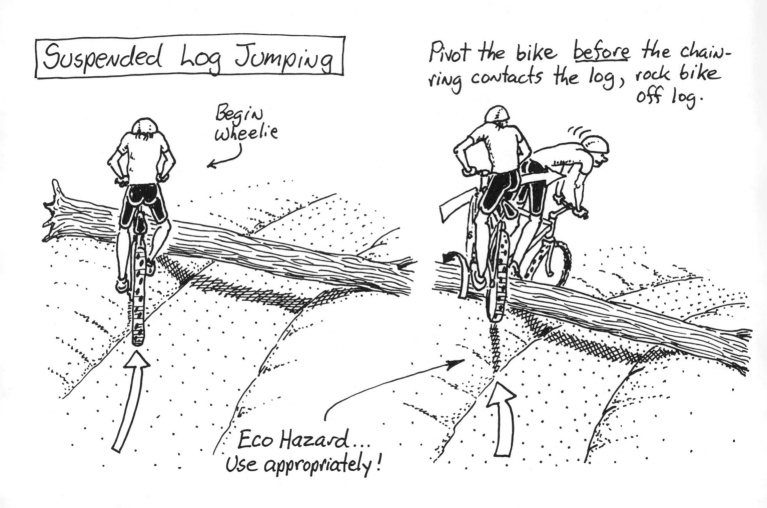

Dab (dâb) v., To touch any portion of one's anatomy to the ground while riding in a trials-like manner. See "face plant" etc.

Limbo Log (lêm·bō lôg) N., (a.k.a. "deadfall", etc.)

A log or other organic obstacle crossing a trail horizontally with several feet of space between log & ground. Misjudge one of these babies, even at slow speeds, and it's ouch-o-rama!

★ Whump! ★   See "clotheslined"

Let your buddy try it
first!

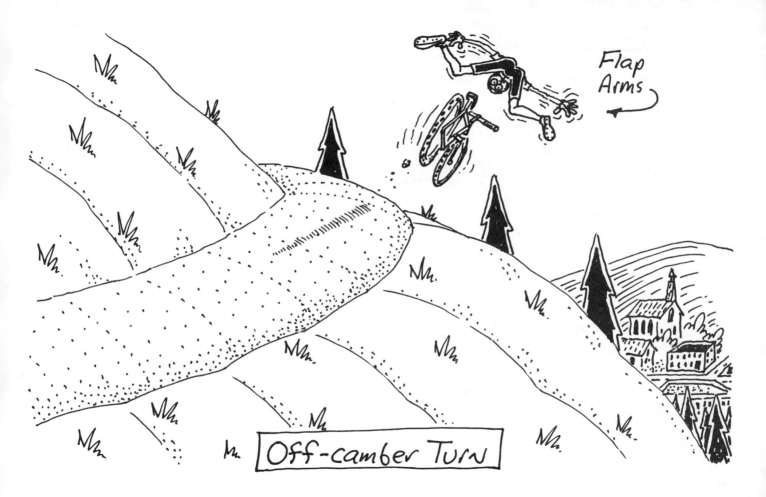

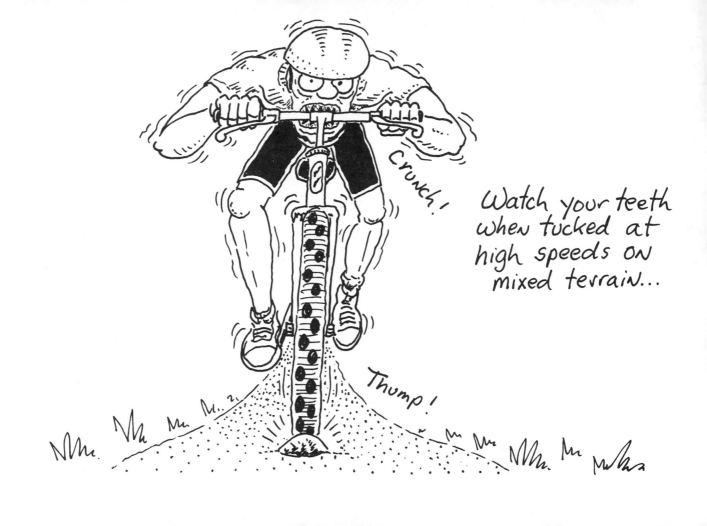

Hammered (hám·mérde) (a.k.a. "crash & burn") Any particularly picturesque total body wipeout with aerial maneuvers. (see "face plant", "body carve", etc. also "first aid")

Aiiiiiiiiieeeee
Nooooo oooooo
Shiiiiiiittt!

The First Winter Descent of the Third or Fourth Highest Peak in the Great Smoky Mountains National Park

After the _Outside_ article on mountain biking appeared in the Spring of '79, my friend Bruce*and I acquired a couple old Schwinns and proceeded to demolish both the bikes and ourselves. Our favorite activities were high-speed pedestrian slalom and staircase-riding on the campus of the University of North Carolina in Chapel Hill. And drinking beer. In short, we were bad boys in need of serious punishment.

That December Bruce, Holly¹ and I drove to Alabama for Christmas via the Great Smokies National Park. Bruce and I

*I can't use Bruce's last name because he's an electrical engineer with a defense contractor now and probably wants to remain so.

¹ see bottom of next page

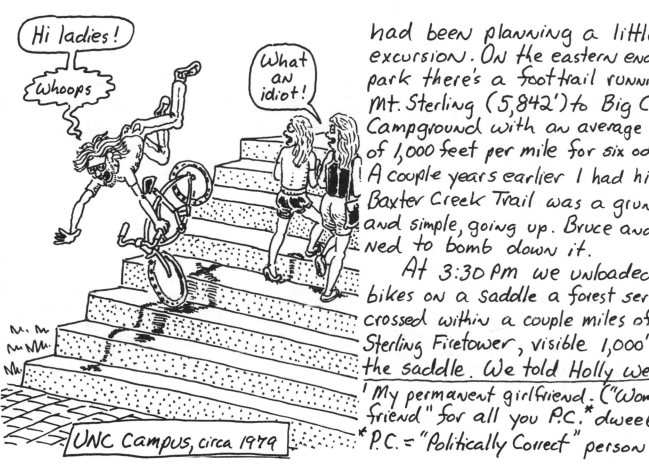

Hi ladies!

whoops

What an idiot!

UNC Campus, circa 1979

had been planning a little side excursion. On the eastern end of the park there's a foot trail running off Mt. Sterling (5,842') to Big Creek Campground with an average gradient of 1,000 feet per mile for six odd miles. A couple years earlier I had hiked it. Baxter Creek Trail was a grunt, pure and simple, going up. Bruce and I planned to bomb down it.

At 3:30 PM we unloaded the bikes on a saddle a forest service road crossed within a couple miles of the Mt. Sterling Firetower, visible 1,000' above the saddle. We told Holly we'd see

¹ My permanent girlfriend. ("Woman-friend" for all you P.C.* dweebs...
* P.C. = "Politically Correct" person

her in an hour or so at the campground in the valley below. Bruce and I figured we'd surely beat the car down. After about 200 yds. the jeep trail to the firetower got too steep to pedal a 1-speed cruiser... we began a push/carry bike ascent epic. At about sundown we staggered into the clearing below the firetower. There was snow on the ground and, because Bruce and I had wisely elected to wear only T-shirts and blue jeans (now sweat-soaked) we were getting very cold. Now all we had to do was to select the correct trailhead to the campground from a number of trailheads leading out of the clearing, all unmarked. Being hippie radicals, we chose the trail-head farthest left. In fading daylight we said a prayer to the bike gods and took off down the mountain. Bruce led because I couldn't see too well in the gloom in my ultra-dark prescription sunglasses. About ten minutes later I slid around a corner and ran over Bruce's arm, which was lying across the trail where Bruce lay sprawled after having been clotheslined by a fallen spruce tree hanging across the trail. After we finally located Bruce's glasses, which had been knocked off his head in the crash, we resumed the descent.

The trail was so steep we had

Whoops... sorry!

Arrrgh!

to ride standing on our coaster brakes, coming down Mt. Sterling in a continuous dynamic skid.

"Mayday! Mayday! I'm on FIRE!" Dense white smoke was pouring out of my rear hub. Neither of us knew exactly what this phenomenon meant. I assumed it meant I was fixing to loose my brake and plummet into Big Creek, a thousand feet below in the shadows. Ulp.

As we resumed our semi-controlled skid down Mt. Sterling we began to speculate on ours and Holly's fate. Being as it was dark, below freezing and we were way overdue, Bruce speculated, Holly has probably begun to think seriously about finding

a ranger and organizing a res-
cue party. If she hasn't been raped
and murdered by the local mutants,
I countered. If we had chosen the
correct trail at the top (and therefore
weren't hopelessly lost and hypothermic)
then, technically, we were merely late
and hypothermic. Surely the rangers
would only fine us and not cart us
directly to a mental institution...

At around 6:30 PM we crossed the
swinging bridge at the campground.
No Holly, no car, no rangers. Shit!
Bruce remembered that, it being late
December and all, this end of the
park was closed until April. It was
two more miles to the entrance gate
and we went real fast.

A vision of Beauty awaited us at the gate: Holly, warm car, cold beer and no rangers in sight. "You are late late late!" Holly said after opening her window about two inches. She took a sip of a steaming cup of coffee and scotch. "I thought you guys were hurt or lost or dead." "Please unlock the doors... pleeeaaassse!" I whimpered "Bruce and I are both very sorry and awfully cold to boot. And we will never even _think_ about doing anything like this ever again!" "Amen" said Bruce.

She started the car. "See you two in Birmingham". She put the car in drive. "It is 350 ⊙★⚡! miles to Birmingham" I choked, hanging

You are late late late!

Chatter Chatter

onto the car with chattering teeth.
"Hmm... 350 miles..." she said
"Well guys, enjoy!"

Epilogue - She eventually allowed two
penitant, frozen mountain bikers into
the car after a little more well-
deserved humiliation. Bruce has a
real job now but rides when he can.
I've become a helmeted, lycra-clad
safety weenie and, between
crashes and injuries, ride in a
responsible and dignified manner.
For me...

The End

P.S. Holly, to this day, refuses to run
shuttle!

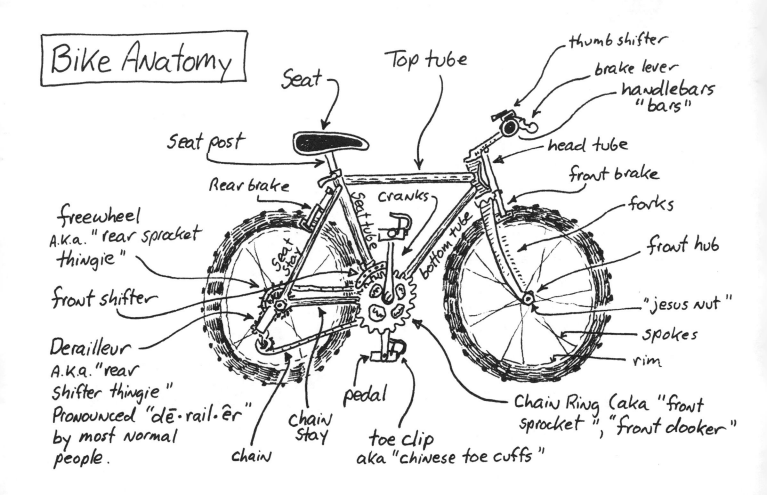

Bike anatomy, cont'd..

Chainring Detail

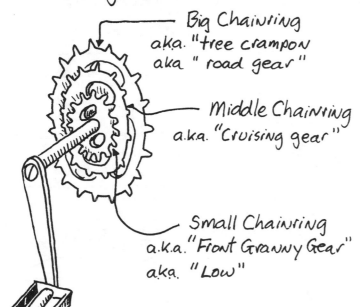

Big Chainring
aka. "tree crampon
aka. "road gear"

Middle Chainring
a.k.a. "Cruising gear"

Small Chainring
a.k.a. "Front Granny Gear"
a.k.a. "Low"

Freewheel Detail
(side view)
A psychometric analysis...

High — low

racer head

regular guy

average dweeb

dweeb

wimp

weenie

"Low-low or granny gear"

Psychometric equivalent based on one's preferred gear under average offroad conditions. The author could be classified as a weenie on the cusp of dweeb

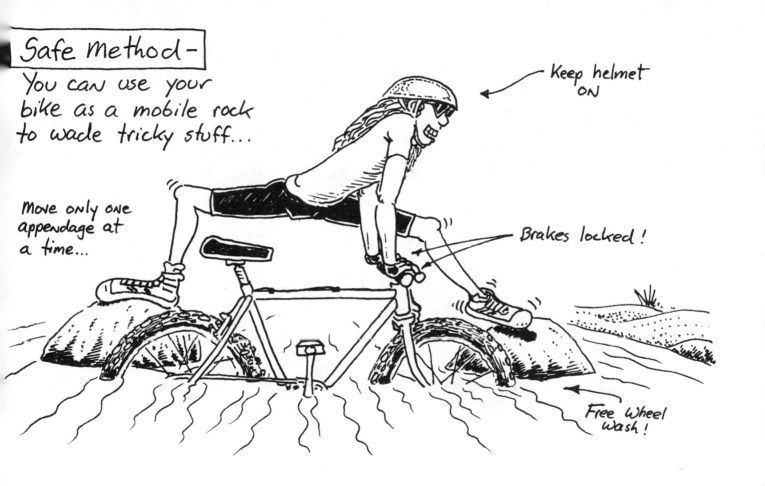

Pedalling Air (pĕd·âl·ng âyr) v., To attempt a hard pedal stroke on a too-low gear thereby loosing one's footing on the pedals, perhaps causing sufficient wobble to crash the bike...

Eeeeeeeee....

Example; bike moving at 5th gear speed. Rider tries to pedal in 1st...

See "beartrapped," & "shift discipline"

Magnetic Turn (mãg·nê·tĭk tûrn) n., A decreasing-radius turn. Inertia will make it seem as if a giant magnet is pulling you to the outside of the turn and over the edge.

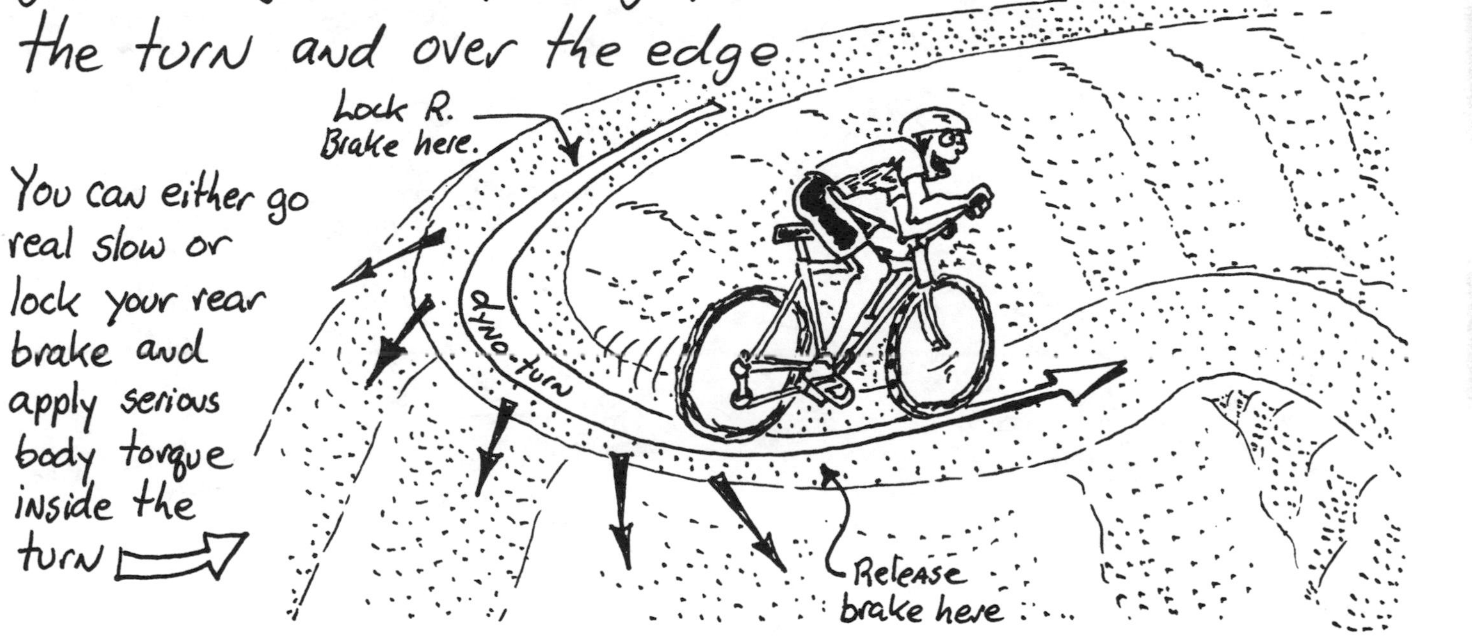

Lock R.
Brake here.

You can either go real slow or lock your rear brake and apply serious body torque inside the turn ⇨

dyno-turn

Release brake here

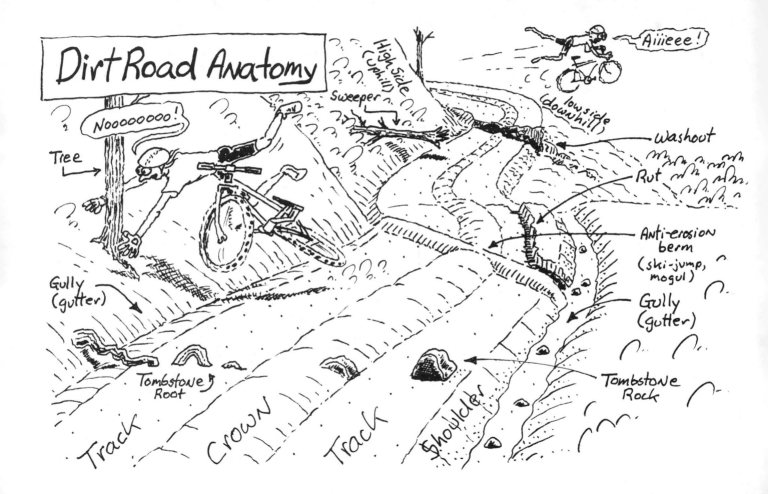

Face Plant (fasê plânt) v., (A.k.a. "head dab," "head plant", "header", etc.) To abruptly establish initial ground contact with any portion of the head or face...

Ask Dr. Conewrench

Dear Dr. Conewrench,

When I ride in the Summer I get a terrible case of scalp itch that even medicated shampoo won't cure. What is the name of this condition and has medical science developed a cure yet?

Tanya
Berkeley, CA.

Well, Tanya, you suffer from a rather common skin ailment we doctors call "Head Rot." Fortunately, there is a cure short of shaving your head and buffing it with a high-speed grinder. After a shampoo & rinse pour about half a cup of Listerine on your head & massage it into your scalp for 5 minutes then rinse. Blow dry if possible. [Editor's Note - Crazy as it sounds, this really works!]

Dear Dr. Conewrench,

I'm always riding thru patches of poison ivy in the woods. Is there any field treatment I should be doing to reduce my chances of breaking out? Also, do you

Know a good recipe for 'possum.
          Bubba
          Fort Payne, AL

  The best field treatment for poison ivy/oak is to wash a.s.a.p. with soap & water. Chances are you won't actually have soap but you should still flush any exposed skin with water from a water bottle or a creek as soon as possible, then soap & water when you get home.
Dr. Conewrench's Possum Delight; You'll need; 1 bottle wh. wine, 2 med. onions, sage, salt & pepper. First drink the bottle of wine. Stuff the dressed 'possum with onions, rub with sage, salt, and pepper. Bake in oven for 20 minutes per pound (about 2 hrs. for a good-size one). After baking, bury the 'possum in the backyard, feed the onions to the dogs & get someone to drive you to McDonalds for dinner.

Dear Dr. Conewrench,
  What is the best treatment for a guy who strikes his private parts on the seat while hopping a log?

          Vanna
          Los Angeles, CA

Dear Vanna,
  Quick painless euthanasia.

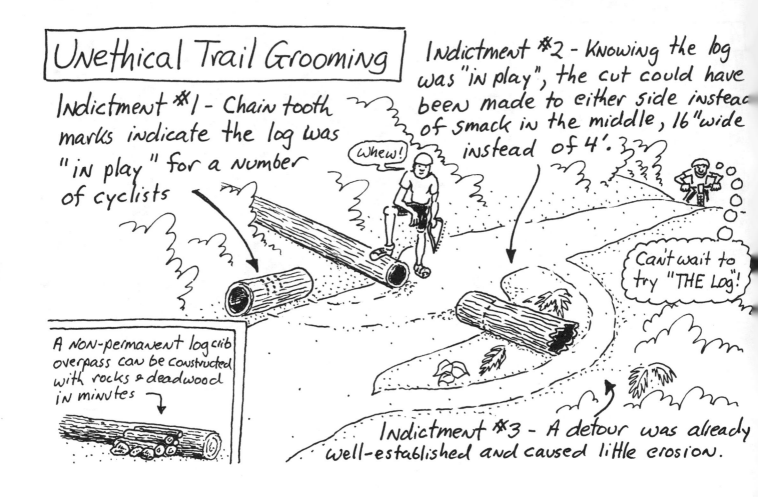

Humor concept by H. Wallace

The History of Mountain Biking..

Despite some of the heaviest bombing in the history of the planet, indo-mountain bikes were used by Vietnamese guerrillas to move hundreds of tons of supplies & matériel south on the Ho Chi Minh Trail each year of the war.

Bad Habit #17

Poor Fred was always forgetting to tune* his bike every week or so. R.I.P. Freddie!

* Tune (tēwn) v., To tighten up & inspect all bolts, nuts cables, connections, etc. etc. at regular intervals...

Body Carve (bôd·ē carv) v., (A.k.a. "Body Slam" etc.) To dynamically come off your bike and do some trenching with your torso...

Ohhhhhhhhhh

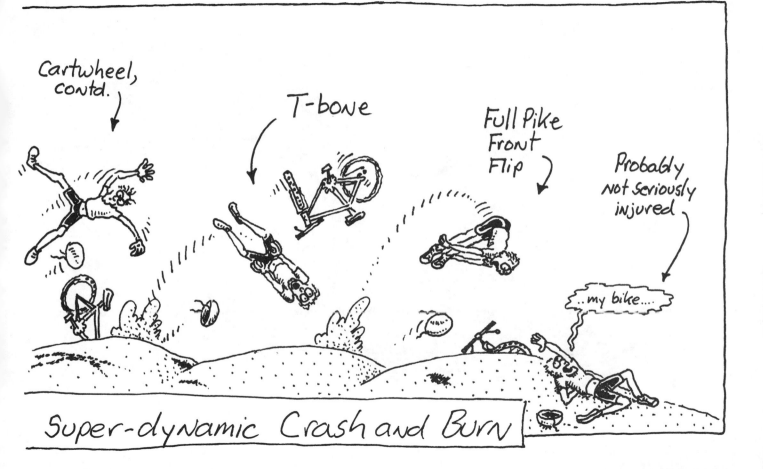

The Ultimate Trials Bike

A Hunting Season No-No

Mtn Biking A.D. 1871

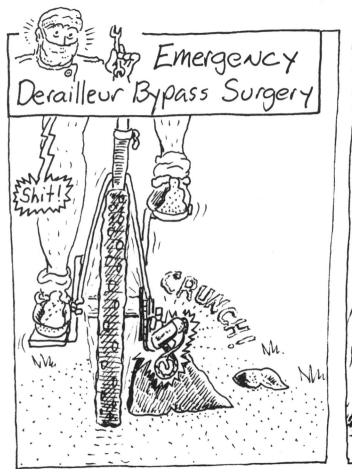

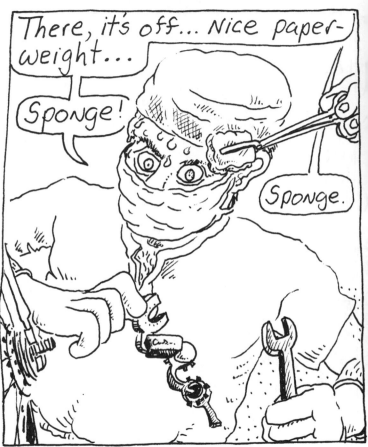

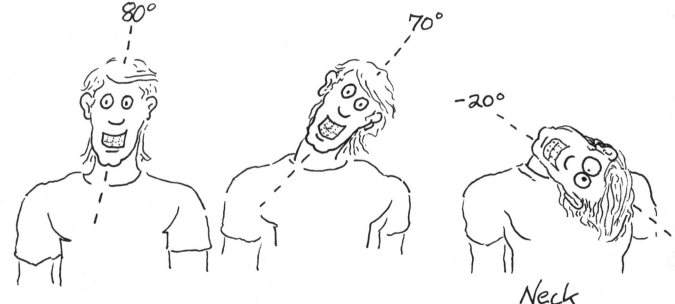

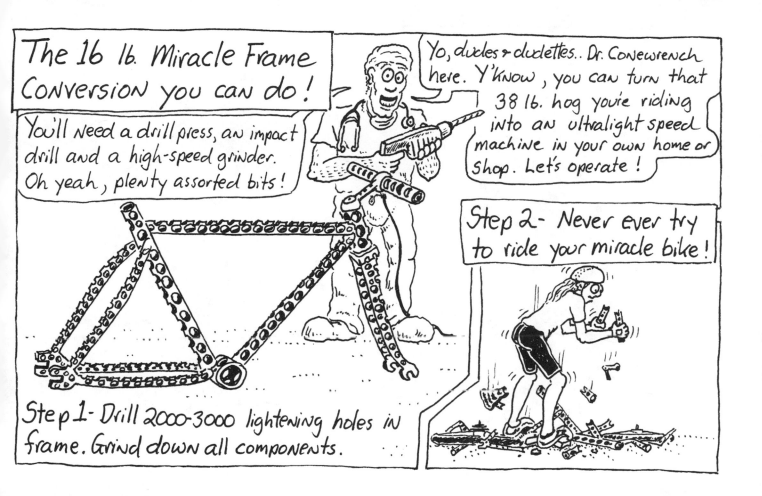

All about Seat Height

Seat too low

Seat too high

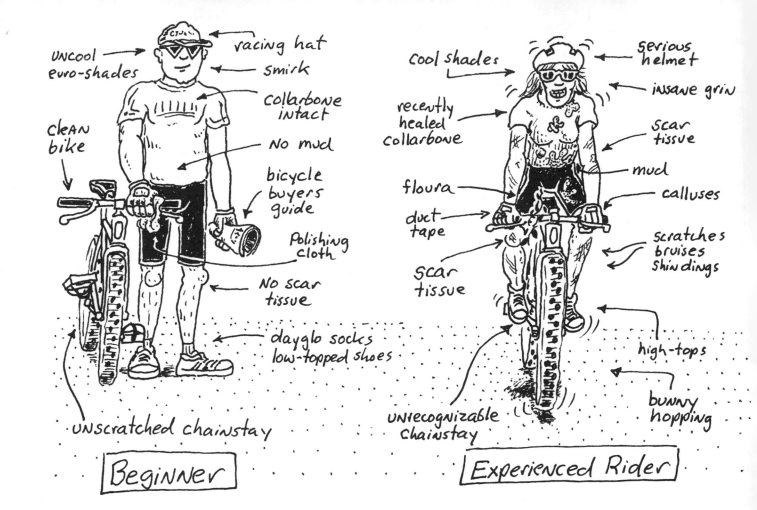

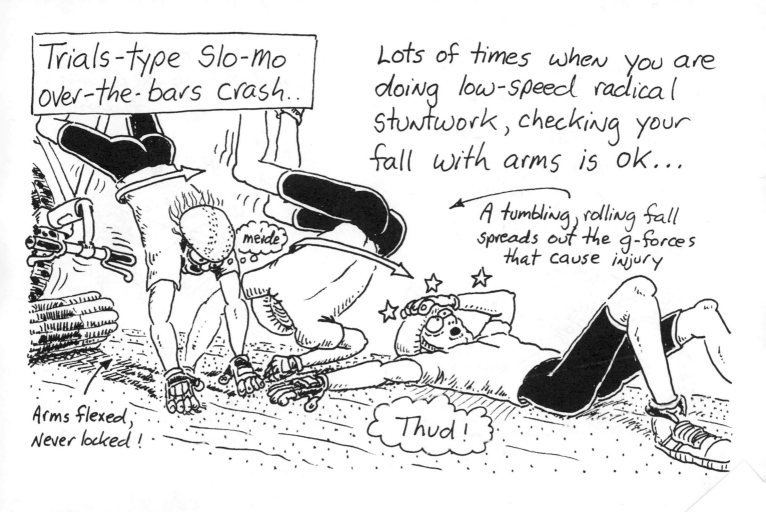

In a high-speed over-the-bars type crash, staying with the bike greatly lessens your chances of serious injury....

... When you go over, arch back, tuck head and think pleasant thoughts...

If you're real lucky you'll do a complete flip and land on the shoulder area of your back and slide...

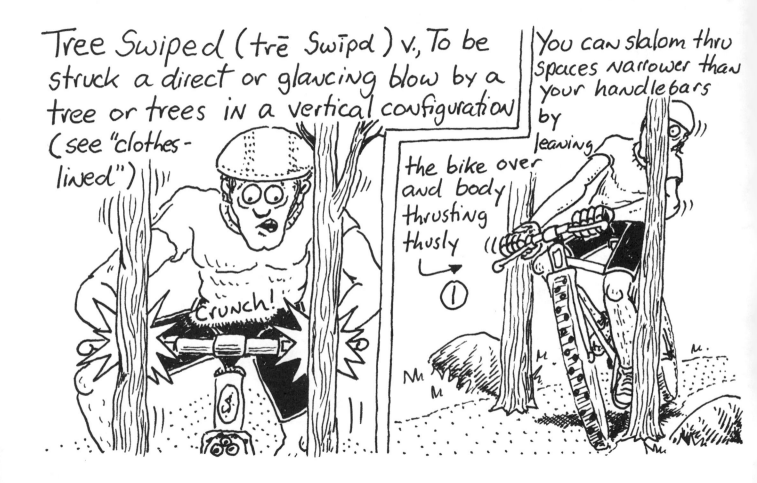

Tree Swiped (trē Swīpd) v., To be struck a direct or glancing blow by a tree or trees in a vertical configuration (see "clothes-lined")

Crunch!

You can slalom thru spaces narrower than your handlebars by leaning the bike over and body thrusting thusly →①

Counting Coup (kôun·tng cōo) v., To lightly tap your polo opponent about his/her posterior area with the handle end of your mallet. This was the Native N. American way of symbolically defeating an enemy without making a big mess...

Clotheslined (clōs·līn·d) v., To be abruptly re-moved from one's mountain bike by a free-standing horizonal object (tree, cable, etc). See "poled".

Event Horizon (ə-vênt hōr-ī-zun) N., Maximum sight distance. As velocity increases, distance to event horizon decreases. (See "First Aid")

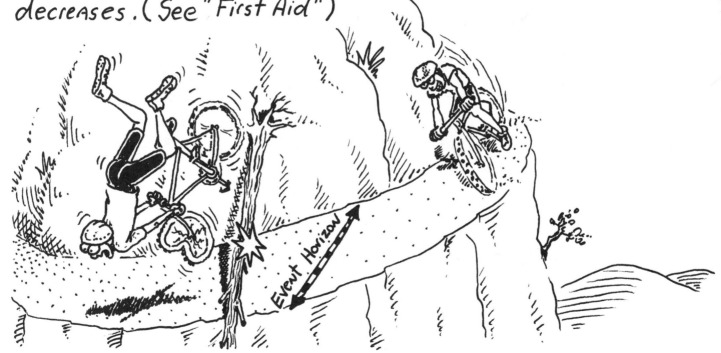

Mudballing (mŭd·bâl·eng) v. To ride in such a way as to become indistinguishable from the terrain...

Wahoooo!

Glurp!

Front-pointing (frûnt·pôint·ng) The art of utilizing the outer chainring as a third wheel to climb over logs and other organic obstacles.

Fun Hog (fûn hâwg) N., Any person having a transient "sports-based" lifestyle with obsessive involvement in any or all of the following outdoor sports: rock climbing, river running, mountain biking, alpine skiing, wind surfing, sky diving, fly fishing, etc. Easily recognized by driving ratty-looking utilitarian vehicles festooned with a vast array of equipment worth at least twice the value of the vehicle itself.

windsurfers

skis

road bike

Kayaks

Climbing Simulator

Typical Fun Hogs

mtn. bike

Assorted gear

Typical Fun Hog Vehicle

Hell Ride (a.k.a. "Bataan Death Cruise", "Exploratory Ride", "Humping the Boonies", etc) A pleasure cruise gone wrong due to misdirection, misinformation, or misadventure. Or any combination thereof.

Bear-trapped (bɔɔr tra·pd) v., (a.k.a. "spiked")
To lose one's footing and catch a bear-trap
type pedal in the leg, usually the shin...

Yow!

Thunk!

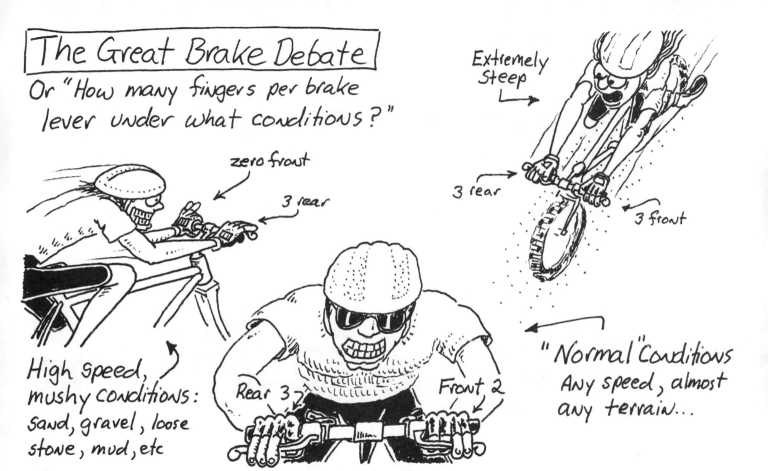

Dog Evasion Techniques

Lesson #1 <u>Always</u> be the rider in front!

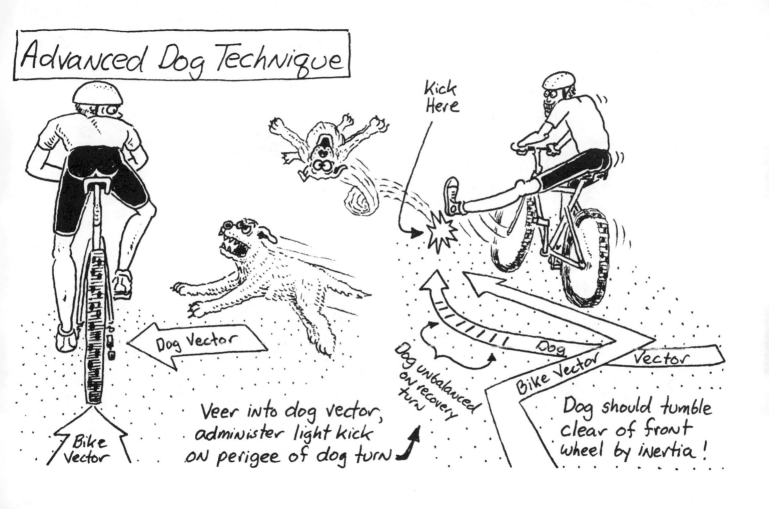

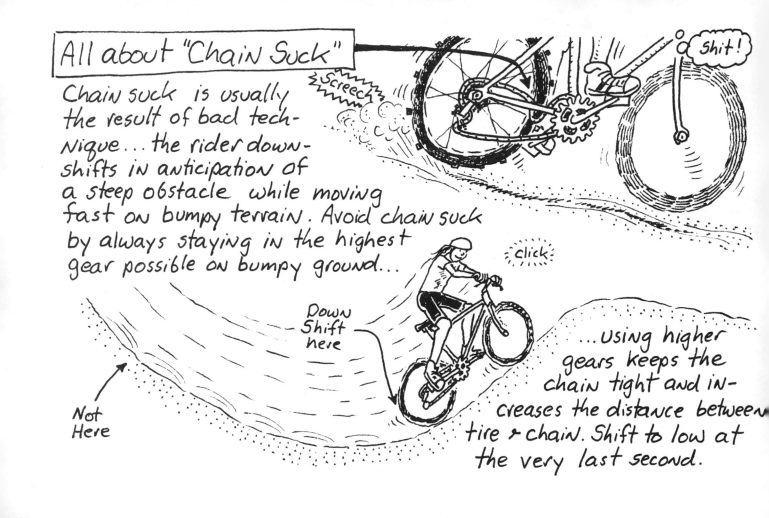

Horse Etiquitte

Mountain bikes are the new critters in the woods. Over time, horses will get habituated to us but right now we are frightening to most of them. In a horse/Mtn. Bike encounter always dismount and give the horse the right of way...

Please Refrain from this!

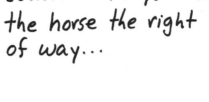

Yo, horse!

Dismount and stand on the downhill side of trail. Stay in horse's line of vision, talk reassuringly. Remount only when horse is at least 100 feet away...

Frontal Approach

Hang well back until horseperson notices you. Usually they will move off the trail to allow you to walk your bike past. Remount at minimum 100' past horse.

Rear Approach

Log Jumping Made EASY..

Large logs (8" to 20" diameter) require talent...

Small logs (4" to 6") can be simply bunny-hopped...

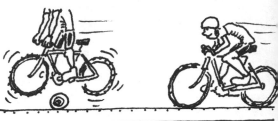

① From a near-stop roll toward log until front wheel nearly touches it...

② Execute a front wheelie and roll forward on rear wheel until chainring hits log...

Foot ready for power stroke

Be ready for hard frame shock when chain ring meets log!

③ Without giving yourself a sex-change operation, stick chain ring teeth in log..
..if you neglected to lower your seat you will now be in great pain!
Watch out for seat!
THUNK!
④ Rock the bike onto the log...

⑤ Pedal over log on chain ring and rock front wheel onto ground...

⑥ Throw weight over front wheel to bring rear wheel over log..

Toe nudge if necessary

⑦ Finish standing with knees flexed...

Caution: if you hit the log too hard with your chain ring (step #3) you get a seat in the Naughty parts. Always go slow & lower seat to jump logs!

Watch that seat!

Thump

OOOF!

THUNK!

A spoke wrench is a dangerous tool in the hands of a neophyte...

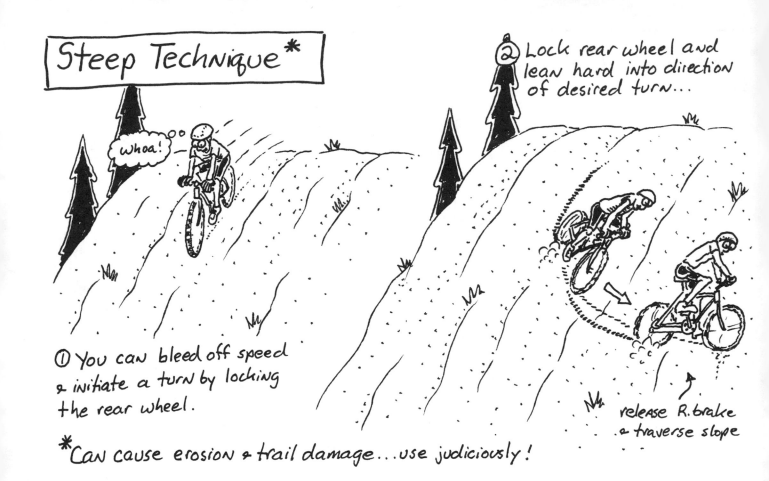

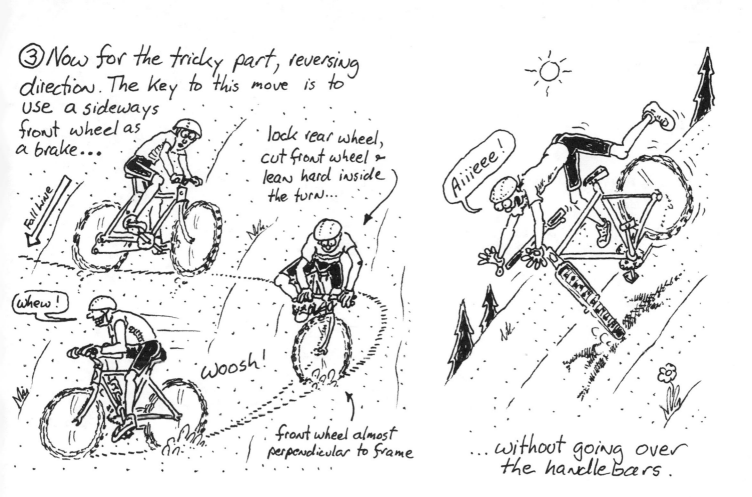

High Speed Rear Wheel Locking Maneuvers; The Dyno-Turn

You can literally carve a turn by locking the rear wheel and leaning to the inside of your desired arc. With practice full 180° dyno-turns are possible..

① Lock Brake Here

② Without turning front wheel lean hard into turn

③ Release Brake Here

Smile for the camera!

pedals level, legs flexed, weight on pedals!

Eco-hazard, Use judiciously!

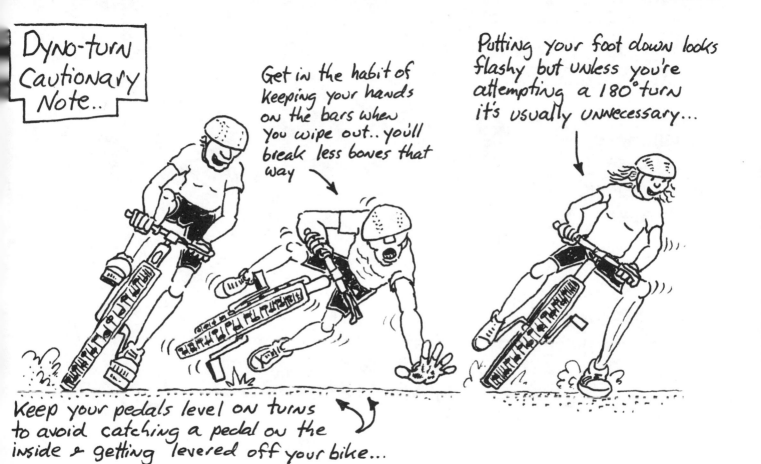

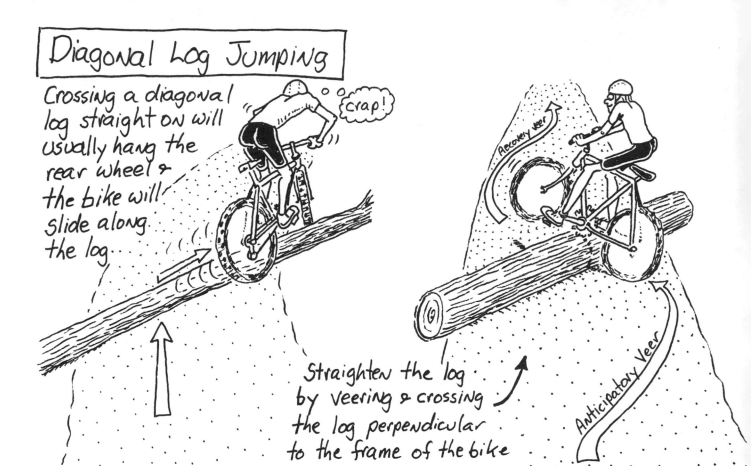

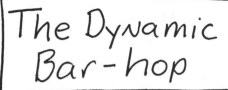

The Dynamic Bar-hop

① *Holy Shi....* o o o

② Warning! If you mess up and get tangled on the handlebars you'll do a dynamic face-dab. This is a low-speed desperation maneuver.

③ RUN!

Wheelie Pivot Turns...

Whereby the rider can make up to a 90° turn in a very small space. This technique is always done from a sitting position and works best on a slight upgrade.

① Shift to Low-Low

Power foot in wheelie position

Body

Torque

② Pop wheelie, apply body torque..

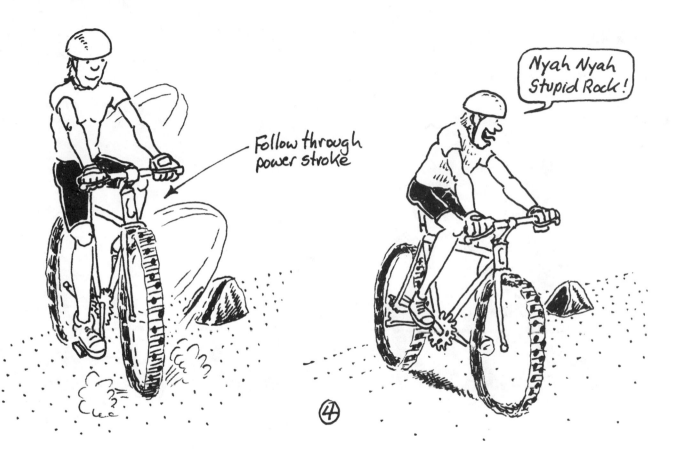

Scootering a Crippled Bike..

If you break a chain way back in the boonies (or pretzel a derailleur, etc.) and lack the proper tools for a road repair don't push your bike, scooter it!

10° to 20° lean

... You use kind of a cross-country ski kick ...

Bad Habit #43...
High speed cruising, body relaxed, 90% of weight on seat. Even a small bump can eject you from your bike.

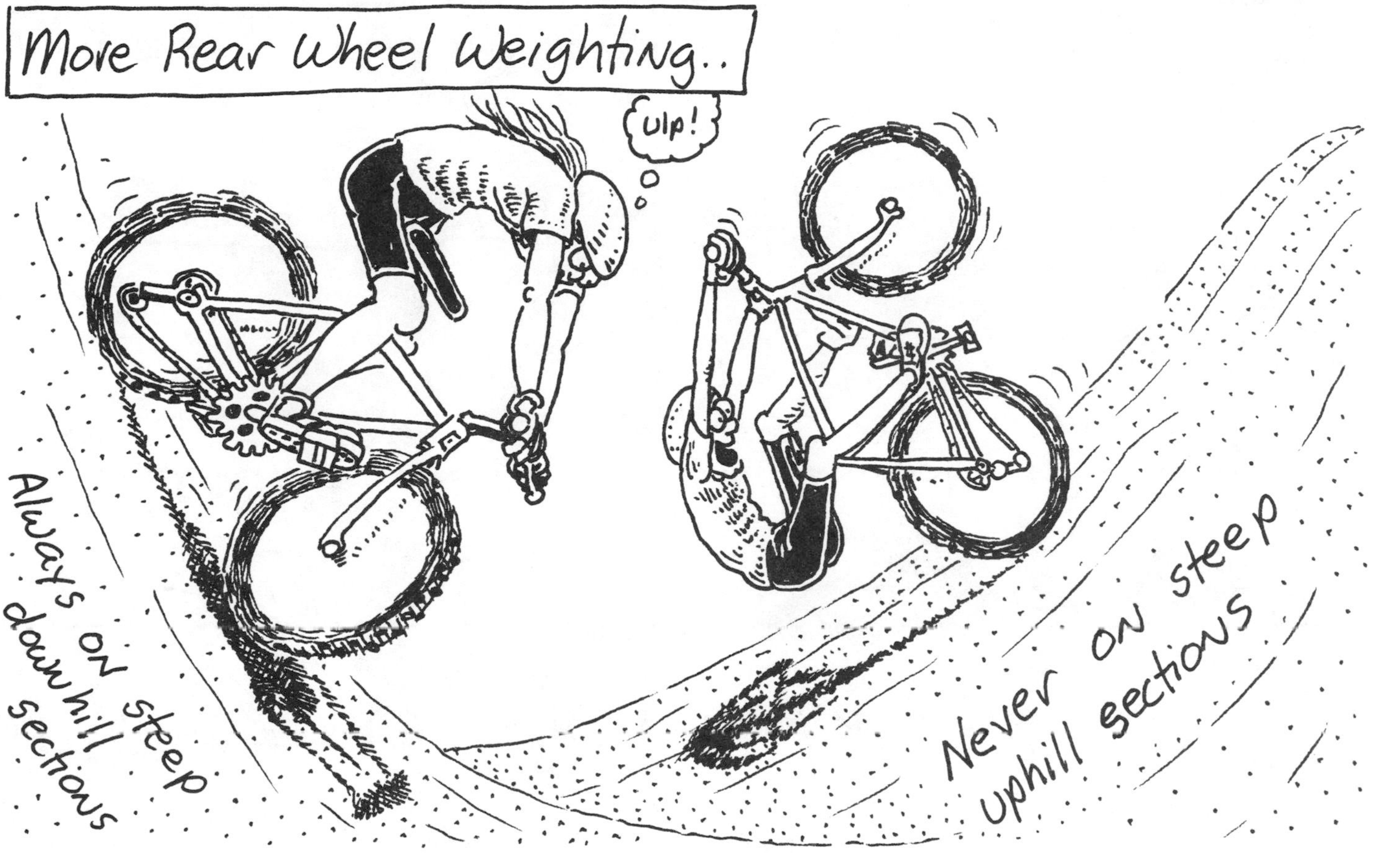
More Rear Wheel Weighting..
Ulp!
Always on steep downhill sections
Never on steep uphill sections

This looks like the place. We'll stash the bikes here in case we need a quick getaway...

Here... put on my wind jacket..

Why?

You're not wearin' a bra... I want to get out of here _alive_..

Oh, OK.. _you_ put on your wind pants!

Do you think I should turn my T-shirt inside-out?

This is INSANE!

Earth First

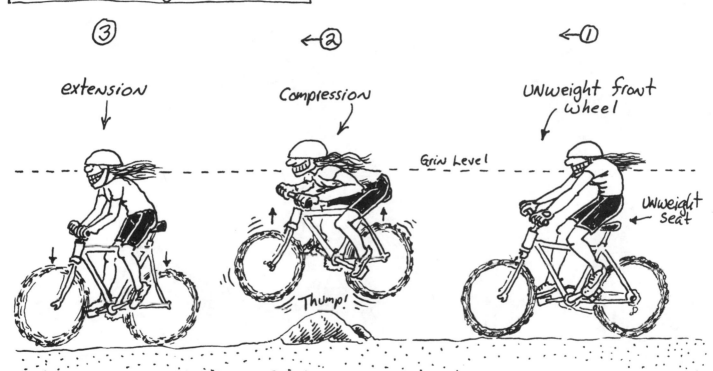

The Future of Mtn. Biking